A CRICKET DICTIONARY

Sun Books Pty Ltd
THE MACMILLAN COMPANY OF AUSTRALIA PTY LTD
South Melbourne, Victoria 3205, Australia

First published by Sun Books 1983
Copyright © Keith Dunstan and Jeff Hook, 1983

National Library of Australia
cataloguing in publication data

Dunstan, Keith.
  A cricket dictionary.

  ISBN 0 7251 0432 5.

  1. Cricket—Dictionaries—Anecdotes,
  facetiae, satire, etc. I. Hook, Jeff, 1928–
  II. Title.

796.35′8′0207

Set in 14 pt Vladimir by
ProComp Productions Pty Ltd, Adelaide
Printed in Hong Kong

A CRICKET DICTIONARY

BY KEITH DUNSTAN
ILLUSTRATED BY JEFF HOOK

SUN BOOKS • MELBOURNE

All Rounder

A

Adelaide Oval	Only Australian ground that sports a cathedral. Often badly needed.
Agricultural Shot	Stand with your feet wide apart. Hold your bat high like a double-bladed axe. Close your eyes then swing. Superbly effective in one-day cricket.
Allrounder	He can bat, bowl, field a bit and in a case of dire emergency probably even earn his own living.
Amateur	Endangered species, almost extinct. By careful examination some rare specimens can be found, usually 12 years old, playing in the war memorial park for St Ignatius, F grade.
Appeal	A 250-decibel scream made to overcome the obvious congenital deafness so common in the umpiring profession.
The Ashes	Charred mess of doubtful origin residing in an old urn somewhere in the Long Room at Lord's. The Poms won't part with them no matter how many Test matches Australia wins.
Autograph	An unreadable scrawl, quite valueless, for which some moon-eyed kid will wait outside a dressing room for anything up to 24 hours. After it is signed he swops it, plus four Englishmen, two Indians and a Pakistani for one Greg Norman.

Appeal

Avagoyamug	The mysterious, almost religious chant that comes out of the mouth of the cricket spectator. Sometimes it can be repeated by the one person 1200 times in an afternoon, especially if the Englishmen are batting.

B

Back	Part of the human skeleton. A remarkably inefficient instrument which is incapable of supporting fast bowling over a long period. Fast bowlers invariably go in the back first then in the knees. If they were horses someone would take them out and shoot them.
Back Foot	Listen to Alan McGilvray and you would swear 95 per cent of all balls were hit off the back foot. Untrue. Batsmen use a bat at least 50 per cent of the time.
Bails	The nice little bits of furniture that go on top of the stumps. The umpire carries them in his pocket and very delicately he places them in position. He takes pride in the way he lines everything up making sure it is square and perfect. One ball later the wicket-keeper smashes down the stumps with a wild stumping foray. The umpire replaces them, taking pride in making sure all is square and perfect. One ball later the wicket-keeper smashes down the stumps again. The umpire replaces them, taking pride in making sure all is square and perfect. One ball later the wicket-keeper smashes down the stumps again. The umpire . . .

Bankruptcy	The price of a new captain and an imported West Indian fast bowler.
Banners	So much noise is evident now in one-day matches, even if a barracker has a brilliant comment it is impossible to make himself heard. Therefore since 1982 there has been a remarkable rise in the popularity of the poster or banner. Posters now cover all the parapets round the stands with such thought-provoking remarks as, 'THE KIWIS HAVE LOST THEIR POLISH' or 'ALL POMMIES ARE BASTARDS'.
Bat	A refined wooden club often used as an instrument to lean upon by the gentleman at the non-striker's end of the pitch. It also doubles as a crutch for injured players, a missile against streakers, a fly swatter, and occasionally an instrument for making runs—except by Geoff Boycott. It can cost anything up to $200 and is usually anointed with linseed oil for an all-over tan. Don't tell a soul if it is made of aluminium.
Batsman's Paradise	A land where the beer is free and cricket has to be played only one day a week. Actually a batsman's paradise is a pitch with all the personality of Tutankhamen's tomb. It is a humorless, lifeless thing. It foils not and neither does it spin. Bouncers from the world's fastest bowler come through as high as a fox terrier's eye and on a clear day you can make runs for ever.
Bay 13	An area at the Melbourne Cricket Ground and one of the most richly vocal spots on earth. Occupants have a strict dress sense—shorts, bare top and thongs. They have a sense of beauty—every passing female must be

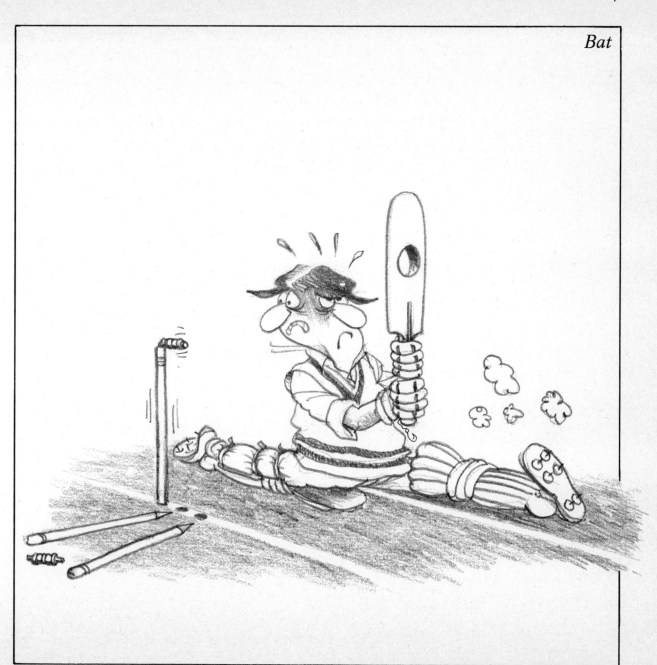

howled at. They have a flair for a gourmet diet—meat pies must be injected with a hypodermic of tomato sauce.

The scene reaches its tempestuous climax in the afternoon as the shadows are moving across the ground and the famous products brewed nearby are having their effect. It is then that Bay 13 starts to bay its awesome menacing chant . . . LILL-EE . . . LILL-EE or more like now LORE-SONN . . . LORE-SONN. You can hear it 20 kilometres off when the wind is blowing the right way.

Bean Ball	Doesn't touch the ground. It leaves the bowler's hand and goes straight at the batsman's bean in an attempt to make him a has-been. It is considered unfriendly.
Block	Taking block, a slow, painful ritual involving an incoming batsman, the umpire and a little pitch excavation. A means for postponing the fearful onslaught.
Bodyline	A picturesque style of bowling which caused an international incident in the 1930s and now is as common as mosquitoes in February.
Bosey	A left-hander's googly. The leg spinner, using the same action, drops the ball on the same spot and it breaks the other way. It caused considerable surprise in March 1902 when B. J. T. Bosanquet bowled the first bosey in Australia. Victor Trumper had scored 40 runs in 20 minutes. Along came the bosey after two delightful leg breaks which were belted into the covers. Mr Trumper looked around. No longer did he have a middle stump. It went the way of his good humour.

Bouncer

A perfectly legal form of mayhem designed to boost the sale of helmets and armour. In its purest form the bouncer hits the pitch half-way down and then rises superbly so that it is heading straight between the batsman's eyes. It is a most interesting product from a game which has gone into the language as a symbol of fair play and good manners.

Bouncer

Box

Protective device made of heavy-duty plastic usually worn in lower torso region, e.g. middle stump. Introduced to the game by worried wives and girlfriends of batsmen. It has reduced embarrassing on-field agonies and eliminated players with falsetto voices. The box is often seen adjusted by nervous batsmen, especially in close up if you are watching the box.

Box

Bradman	See God. Said to have been crucified by Larwood of the Bodyline but rose again in the Second Test. One parable has a young follower in the Outback listening on his crystal set at 1 a.m. to Bradman hitting the Poms all over the ground in way-off England. Impressed by that miracle happening in the dead of night he was heard to say, 'Cripes, if he's doing that when it's dark, think how good he'd be in the day time.'
Bump Ball	You have waited six solid hours to see a wicket fall. Suddenly through your drowsy daze point takes a brilliant one-handed catch. The batsman doesn't move. The umpire turns away thinking of his tea. After six solid hours a bump ball is a terrible thing.
Bye	A way of scoring a run or more by cleverly missing the ball. The umpire raises one arm as if he wants to leave the room. The wicket-keeper wishes he could.

C

Call for a Quick One	Batsman desperate for a drink.
Capped	In football you win a guernsey. In cricket you get capped. Except they're not wearing them so much any more. Maybe you should be hatted or helmeted.

Catch

Captain	He should be good-looking, charismatic, a diplomat, capable of winning arguments with his fast bowlers and should he drop his pants at the Adelaide Oval he should do it with a certain panache. He should be superb at after-dinner speeches and capable of handling with ease curly questions at press conferences. He should know as much about strategy and tactics as a Field Marshal and be a master of psychological warfare. It is a help if he can bat and bowl.
Castle	One has a castle, exquisitely put together. It is composed of three stumps and two bails. Precisely like sand castles at the seaside inevitably it succumbs to irresistible forces.
Catch	Happens when one round irresistible force meets an immovable five-fingered object. The ultimate humiliation for a human being is to stand near the boundary fence before 90 000 spectators, plus another 20 million looking at their coloured TVs around the world and . . . and . . . and drop the bloody thing.
Caught Behind	Trapped in the turnstiles.
Cherry	Once upon a time, the true cricketer wouldn't talk about the ball, he would refer to the cherry. Indeed the redness of the leather ball was one of the great features of the game. It was important to keep the shine on the cherry, so relentlessly they would polish it on their trousers leaving a red stain down the front. Wives and girlfriends of fast bowlers who did the laundry led very difficult lives. Now for one-day cricket they have a strange white thing which leaves no stain. What do they call it? The white onion?

Chinaman	A chinaman is a ball bowled by a left-handed spin bowler whom batsmen would cheerfully deport to China. He would be the only left-handed spin bowler amongst a thousand million people there.
Chucker	Call a man illegitimate, a liar, a cheat, a thief; suggest he is unfaithful to his wife but to describe him as a chucker, one who throws the balls, that's going too far.
Clipped off the Toes	See Back Foot.

Clipped Off the Toes

Close the Gate	Put up the shutters. Bring down the curtain. A style of batting worshipped by those who believe one-day matches are ten days too short.
Commentator	He's venerable. His eyesight is not as good as it was in 1938 but it's remarkable how he can still pick an inswinger or an outswinger from 200 metres. What's going on in the centre can be a wretched inconvenience when he's just recalling that marvellous incident on the fourth day of the Fifth Test at the Oval in 1948. He is superb at describing seagulls and most graceful when at 5 p.m. he refers to the long shadows moving across the ground. At 6 p.m. during the summing up he can usually cause a shock by actually referring to the day's play.
Covers (1)	A position occupied by a human safety net who runs like an Olympic champion, cuts off those red-hot cover drives that were meant to go straight to the fence, or takes catches sprinting forwards, backwards, diving and leaping. Most of all he is chosen for how he will come up on TV action replays.
Covers (2)	A pitch is a sensitive, overworked creature that must be kept warm and dry at all costs, therefore a blanket is provided. Like most blankets it spends an unbelievable amount of time coming on and off.
Cricket	Pronounced 'Crikk-itt' in England and 'Criggit' in Australia. Like living in igloos, skate boarding and eating tripe, unless taught at birth it remains for ever as unfathomable as nuclear physics.

Covers

Cutter

Curator	He has been preparing Test wickets for 35 years and he learnt the trade from his father. He knows how to weave spells. He knows the magic ingredients of right soil, grass, correct watering, plus rolling to bring it to ultimate perfection . . . for a victory by the home side.
Cutters	The book says cutters are easy. You grip the ball with the seam between the index and middle fingers. Then just when you let the ball go you simply pull your fingers across the top of the seam, which makes it turn the moment it hits the pitch. Sometimes it works on Shrove Tuesday or Michaelmas Day.

D

Dancing Down the Wicket	One never walks down the wicket. In the noblest ABC terms one either advances or dances. Undoubtedly the tango or the modern waltz would be the most picturesque.
Declaration	Declarations of independence, very common on the cricket ground. For gentlemen like Dennis Lillee or Ian Botham thay can cost anything up to $1000. Other sorts of declarations mean that you are pretty darned cocky. You've got the opposition in the palm of your mitt. With a bit of luck you might even get home a day early.
Deep Fine Leg	Peace on earth and good, tall women.

Dancing Down the Wicket

Dig In

It is most unseemly for an opening batsman to do anything rash. In a Test Match he might consider after the ninth or tenth over whether he should play a stroke or even score a single. He digs in.

Dig   In

Draw	The battle goes on for five days in stifling 40 degree temperatures. It is estimated that the fast bowlers between them have done the equivalent of two marathons and the century makers each have run eight kilometres. The combined crowds meant 230 000 through the turnstiles. Twenty-five million on both sides of the world watched it through television. The various advertising contracts were worth 5·2 million. The media have produced 1·9 million words. Relations between the two countries have raised comment in the respective Houses. It was a draw.
Draw Stumps	A dentist is needed.
Drinks	Back in the grand old days of big cricket the gentlemen of the game always were supplied with champagne. There was almost a strike when this sound restorative was abolished by the wowsers in the 1880s. Now drinks come out on a trolley after one hour's play and it's a chance to see what the 12th man looks like.
Drives	Tend to be 'superbly controlled', 'full blooded', but in 'full flood' they are 'majestic' and 'rattle the pickets.'
Duck	A blob, a quack, a zero. It derives from the noise, the insolent mirth quacked by this absurd bird. The Japanese with their clever electronic instruments have magnificently aided in the humiliation of failed batsmen. One can now get an electronic duck against a batsman's name on the scoreboard. But the ultimate in batter degradation is provided on television. As the batsman leaves the ground the machine depicts a little electronic duck plodding behind.

Drinks

Duck

E

Ear Plug	A most useful invention. In the members' stand where noise is unthinkable some gentlemen sit with plugs in their ears so that commentators can advise them on what they are looking at. Ah, but the chief advantage of an ear plug is so that you can lie in bed at 3 a.m. and listen to play on the other side of the world without your wife growling, 'turn that idiotic thing OFF.'
Edges	Edges are very common and almost a disease. Batsmen suffer from them constantly. You can get a top edge, a bottom edge, a thin edge and incredibly enough a thick edge.
Elect	After winning the toss the captain doesn't merely 'decide' to bat or bowl. It is much more profound to announce that he 'elects'.
Emotion	It is vital as soon as a wicket falls to exhibit a suitable display of emotion for the TV replay. The bowler gives a tribal scream and leaps three metres into the air throwing up both arms. It is helpful also to throw out a clenched fist. If it is a catch then the catcher must throw the ball vertically above his head to exhibit the triumph. He must be careful though to recatch it as it comes down. After this first ritual all those associated with the dismissal must be embraced and hugged. It is not essential to kiss the bowler, but most do.

Emotion

Esky

A trade device used for carting refreshments mostly into sporting grounds. Many of them are made of plastic foam. In moments of extreme emotion during Test matches it is done to break up your Esky and throw the pieces at other emotive creatures.

Esky

Extras	Or in politer circles, sundries. Here we have the collection of no balls and byes. Extras is quite a fellow. Sometimes he is so skilful he is the top scorer for the day.

F

Farming	Opening batsmen are devoted farmers. It helps dispel terror when the 160 kph monster at the other end is out to kill. After each ball he walks down the wicket and pats down the imaginary bump with the base of his bat. Also he gives a little sweep here and picks up a piece of grass there. Ken Mackay kept the tidiest farm you ever saw.
Fast Bowler	There is silence as the tall, lean man paces out his 30 metre run. He'd go further except that he'd have to pay every time he came through the turnstiles. He limbers up, rolls over his arm and does a few push-ups as part of his psychological warfare. The crowd starts to chant his name, louder and louder as he approaches the wicket. He lets the ball go with a head-high bumper. 'No ball', drones the umpire. The awesome gentleman says a word that even the most innocent can lip read on television and he starts all over again.

Fast Bowler

Father

As soon as the lad is old enough father gets him his first bat. He shows precisely how to embalm it in linseed oil and the house reeks once again with the glorious evocative odour. There are other great birthday moments, the first batting gloves, the first pads. It is noticeable that father is curiously hard to find at the office on Wednesday afternoons. He is reliving his disappointing past and it is pure bliss the day Junior makes his first fifty with the school XI.

Father

Field Placings	Silly mid off, silly short leg, long leg, square leg, mid wicket, slip, point, long on, cover, gully, deep square . . . curious places for human beings to stand for long periods in the hot sun. Obviously invented by a Chinese-born Irishman in Middlesex on 1 April 1720.
First Wicket Down	You're supposed to be the most brilliant stroke player in the camp. The openers are there to take the meanness out of the quickies, then in you come to do the dashing stuff. But it never works out that way. Inevitably they get an early break through and within five minutes you're just another opener. The smart old hands always come in around number four.
Flag	An essential part of the spectator's equipment. A flag waver works like a drover's dog. The great national flag must be waved after every daring single, after every catch, after the fall of every enemy wicket. He gets a rest when the opposition does something wonderful. Then he doesn't wave it at all.
Flannels	To receive one's flannels meant that you were promoted to the school team. Cricketers also were known as flannelled fools. Now they are mostly polyestered fools.
Flash	The air is humid, the medium-paced quickie is bowling outswingers that are bending all over the place. You are swinging and missing. In other words you are flashing outside the off stump. Or to put it in commentators' language, you are hanging your bat out to dry.
Flies	Beloved creatures indigenous to Australia. They adore sportsmen. They like to settle on a batsman's nose or

hum around a fieldsman's head as he is composing his thoughts for a catch. Australians would hate to be without them. The dreaded Douglas Jardine was swatting away one afternoon at the Sydney Cricket Ground when a cry came from the Hill, 'And keep your bloody hands off our flies, Jardine.'

Flies

Football

Follow On	Your opponents knock up 400 runs. You make 85, so you are invited to follow on. Always 'invited'! Like hell. You don't have any choice.
Football	A crude winter game played with an inflated pigskin. It provides much tedious talk in the newspapers, bars and on the air waves. If particular care is not taken it will get worse and the desire will arise to play it all the year round.
Full Toss	A gift from God, as nice as finding a ten dollar note on the footpath. It should be picked early and sent swiftly and gracefully over the fence. Regrettably it usually arrives when your dopey first wicket down is wondering what's for dinner and he's clean bowled.
Furniture	If you are aiming to become a commentator rich in style and metaphor, then don't come out with the crude line that the batsman has been clean bowled. The striker has had his furniture disturbed.

G

Gabba	Short for Woolloongabba, the home of cricket in Queensland. You can bowl from the Vulture Street end which always seems to have a charming air of menace. One time it was surrounded by Poincianas and wonderful Moreton Bay figs. Now it is surrounded by a dog track. It is the one cricket ground in the world that has gone to the dogs and prospered.

Gedderbag	This is a friendly cry of encouragement that one gives to a fieldsman when he fails to take a catch.
Ghost	Actually the great man's cricketing talents flowered so early he left school when he was 14, yet he has written three books and his syndicated column which appears in 14 newspapers is full of simile, metaphor and glorious rolling phrase. There's a little fellow who follows him everywhere. He has a battered Royal typewriter in a black box. Every night at the hotel he gets together with the great man around 9 p.m. and they put thoughts together. It's a lonely role. He is the ghost.
God	See Bradman.
Golf	It is the custom for touring cricketers on rest days to play golf. The affinity between the two games is not easily explained. Perhaps there is an interesting lack of logic about both. At least a golf ball is stationary when one hits it, but then it is much smaller and harder to find.
Goodna	Soil used at Brisbane's Woolloongabba ground comes from Goodna. There is also a famous home in the area for the mentally ill. The two are not necessarily related, as is commonly thought.
Goodonya	Vintage Oz-speak for: 'I am particularly satisfied with your performance.'
Green Wicket	The wicket has a lush covering of grass. It's a fast bowler's dream. If you don't possess any fast bowlers, then you get the curator to prepare something more akin to Simpson's Desert.

Gully	Typical bush cricket ground. You can spend half an hour trying to find the ball between silly mid on and long on.

H

Hair Oil	Lubricant favored by elegant fast bowlers. Brylcream was much favored by Keith Miller. Well, what else can be used to get a shine on a cricket ball? It is illegal to bring out a tin of Kiwi.
Hand Clap, Slow	When no runs are scored for 20 minutes in a Test Match, or for a minute and a half in a limited over affair, the crowd becomes restless. They start a slow hand clap, beautifully co-ordinated, which reverberates through the stands. Sometimes it tempts a nervous batsman into something rash. But on men of immense character such as Trevor Bailey or Bill Lawry it had no effect whatever.
Hats	There is a tradition in the members' stands that if you leave your hat on the seat then you can go away for your pie, beer or cucumber sandwich and return to find it unoccupied. But there is the famous story of the gentleman who returned to find his seat occupied by a North Countryman who said: 'It's booms that keep seats lad, not 'ats.'

Helmet

Helmet	The modern batsman goes to the wicket shielded in armor like a medieval knight. His crowning glory is a helmet with an extra shield of plastic to protect his jaw. The acme of upmanship is to face up to the domestic hurricane for two overs then ostentatiously call for the 12th man to take one's helmet away. Who needs it when they're bowling this slow?
Hook	The ball is advancing towards you at better than 120 kph. If you don't duck it will get you straight between the eyes. The alternative is to hook. You swing the bat around across your shoulders in a splendid horizontal arc. It is tricky stuff, so easy to get an edge, so easy to bounce a catch. With a little bit of luck the ball either goes over the fence or it hits one of those advertising signs as if it has been shot there. Alan McGilvray drones over the radio: 'Rash. I wish he wouldn't do that sort of thing so early in the innings.' In the Outer they are going berserk, waving their flags as if the 8th Army has just taken Alamein.
Horse Racing	A strange unnecessary sport where horses are thrashed into competing against each other. It is used for the sole purpose of interrupting cricket descriptions on the radio.

I J

Index Finger	A useful instrument on a human being. It can be pushed into a hole to hold back the flood in dikes in Holland; good for scratching one's nose and marvellous for holding a fountain pen. Ah, but when the umpire holds that finger aloft, you are ruined, finished, out.
Jingoist	A devoted fan who believes that perfection is the home side, and looks upon the opposing side with the sort of rich, warm love that an Arab has for a Jew, a North Korean for a South Korean or a Sydney towner for a Melburnian.

K

Kiwis	Occupants of New Zealand, a small country on the way to the Antarctic. It is good for quality carpets, lamb, mediocre beer and terrible wine. For its small population it produces extraordinarily gifted cricketers. Kiwis are sensitive about Australians. Handle with care.
Knock	Something one does respectfully on St Peter's gate to get into heaven. A good knock is similar for a batsman.

Index Finger

L

Late Cut	When it comes off it is the most exquisite shot in cricket. When it doesn't you are a mug galah hanging your bat to dry outside the off stump.
Leg Glance	Tricky shot, best conducted out of the presence of wives and girlfriends.
LBW	A leg placed before the wicket; indeed in most cases two legs. Batsmen use them interminably to stop the ball from hitting the stumps. Don't worry about the rule, the umpire doesn't understand it either.

LBW

Left-Hander	Throughout history a suffering persecuted minority, but in cricket loved and sought-after. Definition of cricket misery: a leftie batting up one end and a rightie at the other. The left-arm bowler also is a treasure, he does everything in reverse. Enlightened mothers, as soon as Junior grabs for his rattle with his left fist, nurture his wonderful deviation.
Leg Bye	One of the strangest gestures. Many still think the umpire just has an itchy leg.

Leg Bye

Long On

Lip, Stiff Upper	An essential ingredient in all those who consider the game of cricket more important than mere life itself. The game is rife with classic tales of noble gentlemen who, rather than let the side go down to ruin, have carried on with coronaries, fractured jaws, skulls, fingers, arms to say nothing of the odd broken leg.
Lolly	A sitter. Sadly they don't come often. It is something the poor bored fieldsman dreams about. The batsman spoons up a lolly. In theory it is easily swallowed.
Long On	Sometimes described as in the deep. Good hearing is not required. Excellent position for detecting the warm, loving comments that come over the fence.
Long Room	A repository for faded cricket bats, faded photographs, worn cricket balls (mounted) that once performed hat tricks, ragged, faded boots once worn by great fast bowlers and antique faded members (unmounted).
Lord's	There is an illusion in many parts that Lord's is thick with barons, earls, viscounts. Actually it is named for Thomas Lord, who originally owned the land and came from humble yeoman stock. It is now the sacred heart, the Valhalla of cricket and making a century on Thomas Lord's plot is every cricketer's dream.
Loyalty	A beautiful old-fashioned emotion which varies in direct proportion to the size of the pay cheque.
Lunch	They get 40 minutes. It's a six to four on bet that it will be ham salad, bread roll, followed by a square of apple pie and weak tea. That's if the poor devil who has been padded up for the past hour is not too nervous to eat.

M

Maiden	Rare in one-day cricket, rarer than sabre tooth tigers in the Outer, but in Test matches maidens being bowled over, very common. Sometimes you get 20 of them before lunch.
MCG	Melbourne Cricket Ground. A vast stadium without a tree or church steeple in sight. Similar to a Roman Circus where Christians used to be eaten by lions and Romans howled for blood. Similar activities take place at the MCG and the summer pastime is howling for the blood of Englishmen.
Member	Creature who has to be put down for the club when he's born so that he can gain a ticket during his lifetime. Upon receiving it he stays at home and watches the game on television.
Merri Creek Soil	The mysterious soil used for the wicket at the Melbourne Cricket Ground and other Victorian wickets. It sets black and hard and looks like overcooked plum pudding. Its ways are varied and strange. Even trained psychiatrists have been unable to explain the behaviour of Merri Creek soil.

Maiden

N

Night Watchman

It's 5.45 p.m. Your star batsman has been sitting padded up half the day. He's so nervous he's just lost his shepherd's pie lunch down the toilet. So to fill in for the last quarter of an hour before stumps you send in one of your mug big-hitting bowlers to confuse the enemy. He's your night watchman.

No Ball

A modern phenomenon. The fast bowler must not have his front foot over the popping crease. The professional quickie may bowl 3000 to 4000 dynamite deliveries in a season but, incredibly, still he cannot judge that 30 metres he charges up to the wicket. Oh, the agony in the Outer. Your champion bowler turns on a brilliant delivery, second slip literally claws the ball out of the air with a catch that looks like a mark taken by a football full forward. Everybody screams, 20 000 flags wave. 'No ball', drones the umpire.

Alternatively, the umpire has forgotten to bring it.

Not cricket

A term to describe any unseemly, caddish indecent behaviour. It can apply to cheating, bad language, dropping pants in public, swearing at the umpire, abusing fellow sportsmen, or crafty, nasty bending of the rules to one's own advantage. How fortunate such things are unknown in the greatest of all games.

Not Within Coo-ee

Early Australian talk for 'we got done'.

O

Off Side	You can smell the oysters for lunch from the other side of the members' stand.
One-Day Cricket	Often described as Packerball in honour of the entrepreneur, Kerry Packer. The batsmen wear fancy dress, they play with a white ball instead of red and the sightboard shrouded in black goes into full mourning. Each side receives 50 overs. Test cricket has a wonderful torpor. It is the one remaining event in the world where nothing happens. You can go to a Test Match secure in the knowledge that here is delicious calm and absolutely nothing will happen until lunch time.

In one-day cricket the openers are chosen for their muscular development and full-blooded hitting power. Fast bowlers bowl to no slips and fieldsmen are spread out on the boundary as if frightened of being hurt. It is difficult to sleep because of the terror of being hit on the head by a six. Non-cricketing people who normally watch blood sports, like football, adore it. |
| **Over** | Six balls in England, eight balls in Australia. Six for one-day matches. In Philadelphia in 1922 they even went for ten ball overs. We have improved since then. Now for a gifted no-balling fast bowler it is no problem to get 18 deliveries in a single over. |
| **Overthrow** | When cover, long on or point tries to bean the wicket-keeper and misses. If well done it is worth five runs to the opposition. |

Overthrow

Pom

P

Patron's Box	It is all glassed in. There is ankle-deep carpet on the floor, an enormous photograph on the wall of a Test in progress, dated 1902. There is a tastefully concealed refrigerator, leather armchairs plus a large remote-controlled television. A waiter serves the drinks and meals, infinitely better than those served to the players, in an adjoining room. If an intriguing event takes place outside in the un-airconditioned raw atmosphere of the cricket match it is possible to toss a gaze in that direction.
Pickets	When a batsman hits a four he always 'rattles the pickets.' Not much chance any more. They are covered with advertising signs.
POM	A term of doubtful origin meaning an Englishman. Many Poms don't like it thinking it is demeaning and derisory. They become even more upset when called Pommie bastards. True, there is a lot of love-hate mixed up in this, but it is mostly love. The truth is we like the word Pom, and we are rather fond of the Poms. As for bastard that also is a term of endearment in Australia as long as the Ocker doesn't put 'dirty rotten' in front of it. Oh yes, we're grateful to the Poms. After all, they invented the curious game.

Popping Crease	According to the rules it is 'a line that must be four feet distant from the wicket and extend parallel with it.' Fast bowlers hardly ever find it.
Professional	He used to retire at 28. He couldn't play the game because of lack of money. Now he retires at 38 through lack of time. He can't fit in all his business engagements and board meetings.
Putting up the Shutters	You should keep the shutters up at least for the first four overs. You should put them up again when they take the new ball. You shouldn't do anything rash the half hour before lunch or the half hour after. Approach your 50 with tremendous care. And getting a century is a most dangerous business. You should play only the safest shots between 90 and 100. Nor should you ever score in the half hour before stumps—you want to be there the next day. Actually there aren't many times when you can let the shutters down.

Q

Queensland	An international side in search of a Queenslander.
Quiet	A hideous awesome thing that comes when the star of the home side has been dismissed for a blob. On grave national mourning days like the morning Don Bradman was dismissed by Bill Bowes for a zero, eerie, shocked quiet has been known to last for five minutes.

Popping Crease

Runner

Quick	If you want to be up with the trends do not say that the opening bowler is fast, always say that he is quick.

R

Rain	Something that happens when you have scored a marvellous 550 runs and you've got 'em cold in the second innings at 7 for 84.
Replays	Your favorite batsman has just been dismissed. It is an event you only wanted to see once. The replay device enables you to witness this excruciating happening six times over.
Riot	Not common in Australia or England but becoming increasingly common in Pakistan and West Indies, particularly if the local side is not doing all that well. You will get a sense of danger when bottles start moving past your ear.
Runner	The fellow who runs off to cash the cheques, buy the sandwiches, borrow the asprins. He also has to run for your heroic star batsman who thinks he has a strained knee.
Run Out	Like many cricket expressions it is as curious as the game. Actually it should be 'slow out'—you ran too slowly. Anyway it's always the fault of the fellow at the other end.

Seagulls

S

Scoreboard

Time was when two rather rotund men stood on a narrow platform and they had number plates which hung on nails. Now the ultimate is a computerised scoreboard. It cost $1.5 million. It is set in the midst of enormous revolving panels which urge you to buy pies, cigarettes and Japanese automobiles. Hard to estimate which of the three is the most dangerous.

The machine is so complex you have to look at it for 20 minutes to work out the score. It is also a television screen four storeys high which provides instant replay of almost every ball that is bowled, so much so the cricketers can watch themselves playing the game. The ultimate indignity is for the batsman making his long walk back to the pavilion. He can see how he went out six times.

Scorer

A human who records on paper every ball that is bowled. Often the scorer is a wife or girlfriend showing devotion that is beyond belief. Doesn't always last.

Seagull

A bird that is extraordinarily interested in cricket. You get them at all cricket grounds. They take up vantage points not far from the wicket and squat as if they were conducting a stop work meeting. Why do they enthuse so much over cricket? There is a theory that when old cricketers pass on they come back a second time as seagulls.

Seam	The leather ball is held together with a seam. It is the seam which makes great swing bowlers even greater. It is cheating to raise that seam with a key or a nail file. You shouldn't even let anyone see you do it with your fingernail.
Selectors	Old cricketers who are getting their own back for the frightful things that were done to them.
Sheffield Shield	You start with the local church team and you are so dazzling that quickly you move into a District side. This is serious stuff, the scores are printed in small type on the back pages and you play every Saturday. In England it would be different, you'd be in a county side and they would play every day. If you can shine in the District XI you may be chosen to play for the State. Now you are in the Sheffield Shield competition—a professional, playing sometimes four days a week through the summer. A strange business. You are watched by a small dedicated bunch of spectators, mainly uncles, aunties, journalists and selectors. Sometimes you wonder where the money comes from to do it all. And always there are fears. In no other job are your shortcomings and failures so immediately and clearly publicised.
Short run	Cricketers are sensitive creative creatures. Unlike footballers they are not easily cajoled into strange ideas of physical fitness. You wouldn't get them out on a short run in a fit.

Sightscreen

A cunning device to irritate spectators to the point of madness. It comes into its full glory when there is a left-handed batsman up one end and a right-handed down the other. Then the sight screen can be moved as often as three times an over, which means all those sitting near the screen have to move. Sometimes they can move their bottoms as far as five kilometres in one afternoon.

Sightscreen

Silly Short Leg
Don't knock them. Lindsay Hassett had two and still performed surprisingly well.

Silly Short Leg

Single	The game is composed almost entirely of singles. According to the broadcasters you usually steal a single and it is surprising how many are cheeky.
Six	An opportunity granted by generous batsmen to allow the spectators to do the fielding.

Six

Sledging — A comparatively new term, but an art as old as the game itself. Batsmen can do it to bowlers, bowlers can do it to batsmen. Wicket-keepers can do it to almost everybody. They are in a lovely position to pass comment. It is simple. You whisper in your opponent's ear words of such loving content he is likely to go berserk or, at the very least, write a full column about you in his syndicated piece the next day.

Slips — Flimsy garments worn by females close to the skin. Remove them and you are in a heap of trouble. In cricket it is a position equally delicate.

Slogger — A bash artist. According to the Oxford dictionary, one who hits very hard with bat or fist. In cricket we try to restrict it to the bat.

Slow Bowler — A creature still common in English county cricket, highly used in India and Pakistan, but in Australia he needs protection. He is being shot out by the selectors.

Smoking — The burning of an aromatic brown weed. Australians have found it a delightful method for financing cricket and most sport.

South Africa — A country which can turn an English, Australian, or West Indian cricketer into a millionaire . . . provided that he doesn't think too much.

Sponsors — Banks, makers of denim jeans, pie manufacturers, insurance companies, tobacco firms, and Japanese car makers who know even less about cricket than Harry Beitzel. Eventually fans and live spectators won't be necessary.

Sportsfone	During a Test match anything up to 20 000 people will become so concerned they will ring up the telephone people to get a recorded message from a flat-voiced bored female who acts as if she is dealing with the rainfall figures, not the dire fate of a nation.
Spring	You are middling the ball with glorious grandeur in the indoor track at the back of the big grandstand. It's a wonderful time full of optimism when you believe this could be your year and even Bradman's records are within your grasp. Not a line about cricket gets in the newspapers, because of the euphoria over football and the first four matches are rained out. That's Spring.
Square Cut	Like the rotary clothes hoist, an extraordinary Australian contribution to world culture. Who else could have invented the square pie?
Square Leg	Battered batter forgot his thigh pads.
Statistics	No other sport has been documented in such detail, probably no other human activity has such a fascinating log of statistics. Not much goes by without creating a new wonderful record. For example, the Reverend Stanton Hollingsfield, made 57 not out on Tuesday. It was the first half century ever scored by a 42-year-old Vicar on Shrove Tuesday before lunch.
Sticky	A sticky, a glue-pot, a joy for the spin bowlers. Stickys were common enough when real men played cricket. Now cricket is such big business there's terror when a cloud passes over the sun. At the first sign of a drop of precipitation the organisation is wonderful to see. Out

come tractors, covers which can be rolled out mechanically and it is all done with the speed of a garage roll-a-door.

Stonewallers	They are not actually stone walls—they just look that way and most of them chew gum.
Straight Bat	A very British term for sound defence. 'The Prime Minister played a straight bat in the House this afternoon.' Some batsmen never learn to play anything else.
Streaker	Creature who wears slightly less than those in the grandstand. Unpopular with batsmen because they upset their concentration. Female streakers upset their concentration more than male streakers.

Streaker

Stroke Player	You don't drink wine, the connoisseurs always 'look' at it. You don't sniff snuff. Gentlemen 'take' snuff. In cricket one doesn't hit the ball. Mate, you stroke it.
Stumped	Captain doesn't know which of his crook bowlers to use next.
Substitute	During a five day Test casualties can run as high as Napoleon's retreat from Moscow. With the opposition's permission it is O.K. to field a substitute. You are considered a cad if you use a substitute who can run 100 metres in 10 seconds and has the catching skill of a six-armed idol.
Super Tests or World Series	An ingenious method which transformed a group of males who had no regular jobs and were seen mostly only at weekends into the super-rich class and slightly better off than the prime minister.
Suspension	Just like footballers cricketers can be reported for vile behaviour. Rudeness to umpires, throwing cricket bats, assault, all these can lead to suspension. Ah, but if your champion fast bowler does something frightful just two weeks before that vital Test Match, it would be safer to let him off with a fine.
Swing	Some clever Cambridge scientists once said it was scientifically impossible for a bowler to swing the ball in the air. Then a batsman replied that any scientist who believed that should try shaping up to Alec Bedser on a damp July morning.

T

Tail	Every team has a tail. Some tails are considerably longer than others. The tail is composed of bunnies— the bowlers, maybe the wicket-keeper, the specialists who were never chosen for their run-getting powers. Frequently they make more runs than the batsmen.
Test	The origin of the name, of course, is obscure. Clearly it is a test of the spectator, a test staying awake, a test finding a good seat, a test parking your car, a test fighting your way through the crowd for a pie, a test of your tired feet, but the biggest test comes when your team is playing on the other side of the world. After five nights with no sleep it is very difficult facing up to work at the office.
Tickle	You get a tickle. Extremely dangerous, particularly when you end up in a slip.
A Ton	A century, a hundred runs, a magic figure, the ambition of every batsman who walks out to the centre. It is extraordinary though how many soar forward, driving, hooking brilliantly through the seventies and eighties, but once they get into the nineties terror strikes them down. They inch forward, nervous single after nervous single. Dare they grasp this awful thing, the ton.

Tickle

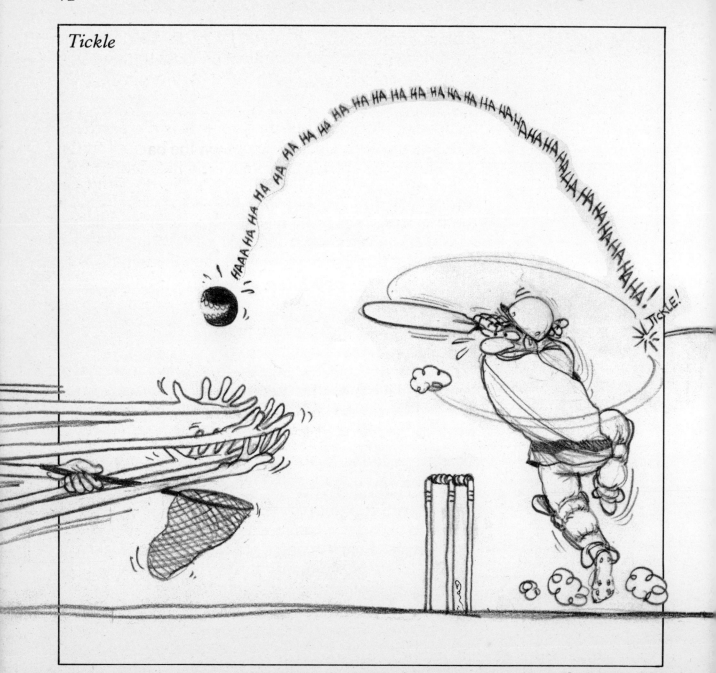

Toofer	It goes wonfer, toofer, threefer, forfer. In the Antipodes we say 'toofer forty', but in the Old Country always it is the other way round where it is, 'Fortah for two wikkits'.
Toss	You bring out your treasured coin. It is a marvellous 1895 penny with Queen Victoria on the back. You flip it up high, the opposing captain calls tails and the old lady comes up. You know there's a faint bit of life in the wicket, so you play a brilliant hunch and send them in to bat. At the end of the day they are 320 for no wicket.

Toss

Twelfth Man

Track	If one is a commentator and acutely aware of modern trends, one never refers to that long piece of turf as the pitch. It is always 'The Track'.
Trot	Batsmen from the poor and indifferent through to the incredibly brilliant all get trots. It has nothing to do with a bowel complaint. It is a mysterious psychological disease. He dries up. Week after week he goes out there and get a blob, while the commentators make merry of his misfortune. He's having a bad trot.
Twelfth Man	The aspiring hopeful. The poor coot can go through six matches and never get into the main side. He runs out with caps, fetches helmets, acts as a runner for the wounded, inevitably fields half the day while the star batsman feels he has an upset stomach or the fast bowler goes off to rest his tired back. He comes out looking nice in his blazer with the drink trolley. He's the poor relation, the bridesmaid waiting to be bride. Contemptuously they call him the drink waiter.
Two Finger Gesture	You can always put the nice interpretation on it. He was only giving the old Winston Churchill V for Victory sign.

U

Umpire	He is paid to be there to decide what happened. He is in an impeccable position to judge. Indeed he is in a better position than anyone else on earth. After he has passed judgement on an lbw appeal or a caught behind

the television cameras will give replays from six different angles and maybe an armchair enthusiast, 16 000 kilometres away, will announce that the umpire is a no-hoper and doesn't know what he is talking about.

Umpire

Underarm   A style of bowling which can be remarkably useful when used against a New Zealander.

Underarm

V

Visor

He goes to the wicket looking like a medieval knight, poor man's version. His visor is made of plastic. Victor Trumper would turn in his grave. Trumper spurned armor to such a degree he wore only one glove. Sometimes he didn't think it worthwhile wearing gloves at all.

W

Wacca

Obviously short for wacky. The cricket ground at Perth is an eternal oven baked to a daily 40 degrees Celsius. The result: A breeding ground for fast bowlers capable of operating in Simpson Desert conditions. The Fremantle Doctor arrives daily at 3 p.m., often too late to resurrect expiring Englishmen.

Walk

You walk when regardless of the umpire's decision you believe it is the right, decent, moral thing to do, because you were honestly OUT. A batsman did walk in a Test match once. It could have been around 1898.

Weather

Something a sport-loving Supreme Being would have abolished. But if it does rain, please God, provide at least 30 minutes of it, so that the club can collect the $20 000 rain insurance.

Wicket	A strange, mystic creature, allegedly 22 yards long. According to some commentators it can even have human characteristics, changing its mood and feeling from day to day. It can be angry, lively at times, pitiless and even remorseless. It can be sticky, it can take spin and oh, too often, when the sun blazes down with 40 degrees heat it can be a corpse of a thing, lifeless, on which bowlers toil hour after hour with no effect. It can be the subject of thousands of words in newspaper articles and often the suggestion is that it should be taken away and buried at sea. At the end of Test play spectators tend to gather round it, and look in awe at this thing which had inspired so much discussion. Some even take home lumps as souvenirs.
Wicket-keeper	The most hideously over-worked member of the team. If he were a unionist he would strike for shorter hours. He handles just about every ball that is bowled and if he drops any one of them the happening makes 10 lines in the morning papers. Then there's the big fellow on the boundary who fancies his arm and likes to get an 'oooh' from the crowd. It comes in three metres over the stumps. Who has to spring back and take a gigantic leap to rescue it . . . the wicket-keeper. He has other duties. As a middle order batsman he is expected to save the side the following afternoon.
Wide	A nice private piece of physical exercise involving the bowler and the wicket-keeper. The batsman can't reach the ball and the wicket-keeper has to act like Nureyev to get it. The umpire makes the classic fisherman's gesture—he extends both arms.

Wide

Wife	A creature who sees her husband a great deal on television. Often she sees his every movement from six different angles, but he's always away from home and she is lucky if she sees her cricketing husband on 100 full days in any given year. And then he brings home half a ton of washing.
Windies	A profound discovery made in the early seventies. It is almost impossible to get West Indies into a three-column headline and they become the WINDIES.
Winter	He never sees anything as horrid as actual cold weather. It is a perpetual heaven of green grass and daylight saving. If he is an Australian maybe he plays his first summer for New South Wales and his alternate summer in the Lancashire League. The Englishman on the other hand maybe is in Lancashire for the Northern summer and Tasmania for the Southern. Naturally he has two girlfriends.
Wisden	The only other publication which records everything with such laborious intensity is Hansard. Wisden's Cricketer's Almanack comes out every year. It was first created by a diminutive fast bowler, John Wisden (1826–84). To own a complete set of Wisden is a marvellous thing, unquestionably more valuable than a complete set of first editions of William Shakespeare.
Writer	Sometimes they are celebrated old players who have gone at the knees, but mostly they are fellows who played as 12th man for the school house XI. Nobody ever offered them a real game, so the next best thing is to write about it and tell the great how to play the game.

X Y Z

Xenophobia	Fear of, or aversion to strangers or foreigners. Very common at Australian cricket grounds where spectators become xenophobic, particularly in mid-afternoon.
Yabba	Famous heckler who fired his wit from the Paddington Hill at Sydney Cricket Ground. Example of a Yabberism:

The umpire raised his hand aloft for the moving of the sightboard. Yabba had a voice as powerful and as comforting as a jet engine. 'It's no use Umpire; you'll have to wait until lunchtime like the rest of us.' |
| **Yobbo** | Until the summer of 1983 he would suffer under the immense loads he would carry into the ground. But according to the latest rules he cannot carry liquor through the turnstiles. Now he can purchase two opened cans at a time.

Yet how fascinating is the remarkable number of cans he can empty in a single day. By mid-afternoon he is knee deep in metal. He has shed his shirt, his shoes, his socks, and his eyes have a dull look. Every three or four minutes he roars for action. Mostly he gets the names mixed and when there's a dismissal, the magic moment is lost because he is sucking on his dummy, his can. It is all a release from the agonies of the week. He is having a lovely time. |

Yorker	You turn on all your clever stuff. You bowl him inswingers, outswingers, you cut them off the pitch, you disguise your pace and bowl him the slow one. Then by sheer luck you drop one into the block hole and . . . goodness gracious . . . you've yorked him. Everyone thinks you're brilliant.
Yorkshire	Cold, damp, flinty place which produces stone walls.
Zaaaaaaaaat	Sir, I have reason to believe that the batsman has lost his wicket.
Zero	Temperature on first day of play at Trent Bridge. See Duck.